Mobile Marketing Madness
For Any Business

I0474029

Learn The <u>Simple</u> Ways To Tap Into A Mobile Marketing Money Magnet for Any Business...

Derby Valentino Perez

© 2011 by Rapid Result Publishing

Steve Kleinman

7 Newark Pompton Tpke

Riverdale, NJ 07457

ISBN- 13:978-1475068535

ISBN-10: 1475068530

First Printing, 2012

Printed from the United States of America

Income Disclaimer

This document contains business strategies, marketing methods and other business advice that, regardless of my own results and experience, may not produce the same results (or any results) for you. I make absolutely no guarantee, expressed or implied that by following the advice below you will make any money or improve current profits, as there are several factors and variables that come into play regarding any given business.

Primarily, results will depend on the nature of the product or business model, the conditions of the marketplace, the experience of the individual, and situations and elements that are beyond your control.

As with any business endeavor, you assume all risk related to investment and money based on your own discretion and at your own potential expense.

Liability Disclaimer

By reading this document, you assume all risks associated with using the advice given below, with a full understanding that you, solely, are responsible for anything that may occur as a result of putting this information into action in any way, and regardless of your interpretation of the advice.

You further agree that our company cannot be held responsible in any way for the success or failure of your business as a result of the information presented below. It is your responsibility to conduct your own due diligence regarding the safe and successful operation of your business if you intend to apply any of our information in any way to your business operations.

Terms of Use

You are given a non-transferable, "personal use" license to this product. You cannot distribute it or share it with other individuals.

Also, there are no resale rights or private label rights granted when purchasing this document. In other words, it's for your own personal use only.

Special Thanks and Dedication

For the people who always believed in me...

My Mom and Dad, they have always inspired me to greatness, there love and support to never give up in what I love... They are the true foundation of my drive, thank you Mom and Dad I love you, always.

My son Antonio, he's the greatest son! Has drive, love and charisma, long walks, laughter and fun will forever be in my heart, he will truly reach his goals and dreams, love you son.

My fiancé Fabi, She always pushes me, supports me, believes in me, when the chips are down, inspires me to never give up on my dreams, her love and strength I will forever hold in my heart...

Special thanks To the Barros Family and Carlito in Vinhedo, Brazil there love, support and a great time in the Country club was priceless...

To all the entrepreneurs and Business people that truly know what cutting edge technology is....

Table of Contents

ACKNOWLEDGMENTS

I would like to acknowledge the following people for their efforts, help and perseverance in helping in my journey to Success, Thank you!

- Rapid Results Publishing - Steve Kleinman

- Carlos Art Nevarez - Wild Horse Performance Marketing

- Maria Gudelis - Wild Horse Performance Marketing

- Tina Williams - Best Refection's Marketing

- Marcus Lee-Crowther - Heaven Sent Media

Introduction to Mobile Marketing Madness for Any Business

More than ever before, small business owners today are faced with a myriad of new and exciting electronic products, systems, and strategies available to them that they can use to increase their business' online exposure. From Facebook to Twitter to video marketing, the list is long and often confusing to the average small business owner.

So as an entrepreneur, you may be asking yourself what is the best, fastest, and most cost-effective way to reach the people in your local marketplace? What is the best online strategy that you can use to generate foot traffic in your place of business, create new customers, and stay connected with your existing clientele?

Even in this dynamic environment, some technologies outshine all others. And today nothing represents a bigger "bang" for your advertising buck than mobile marketing. That's because mobile marketing gives small businesses the ability to reach out and find your potential customers instantly -- whenever and wherever they may be.

So what makes Mobile Marketing is exploding In the USA and it's the #1 choice of many savvy business owners all over the world...and in your hometown? Tap into the Mobile Madness Era!

Well let's have a closer look at some facts:

1.   With today's smart-phones, consumers are accessing the Internet all the time; from work, from sporting events and while watching TV at home. The amount of data flowing across the airwaves is astounding and it's growing at an intense rate. Simply put, if your business is not utilizing mobile techniques then you are just missing out on potential business.

2.   Around the globe today there are roughly 5 BILLION consumers already walking around with a mobile device every day...and that makes contacting these potential customers relatively easy, no more landline phones it's all Mobile and people are always on the Go!

3.   Most people keep their mobile device within arm's reach 24/7. What does that mean? Well the use of SMS Text Message Marketing will result in most of your messages being seen at a glance and read by the mobile device owner. This of course will return higher promotional redemption rates, and bring the possibility of more sales, which in turn could lead to more profits if you can market yourself right.

4.   The average American is already spending almost 3-5 hours per day surfing the Internet from their mobile devices

more the 50% of users are in there smart-phones. These millions of eyeballs represent online traffic that is ready to hear your own promotional message, say good bye to PC and Laptop it's slowly being taken over by Smart-phones, I-pads and Androids.

5.   From a statistical perspective, three years ago in 2009, around half a BILLION people used their mobile phones to explore the Internet. Over the next 5 years this is expected to double! The time is now to implement mobile marketing techniques in your business and mobile detection for mobile websites and Mobile Apps, to reach your Audience quicker, faster and easier.

6.   By 2014, the use of mobile Internet usage is expected to surpass traditional desktop Internet usage. So the use of mobile marketing technology will be critical if you want to stay ahead of your completion and not get penalize by Google search engines.

7.   According to Facebook, more than 200 million users (out of over 600 million Facebook users) access Facebook using their mobile phones. In addition, customers accessing Facebook from their mobile devices are twice as active as non-mobile users.

The above facts indicate that if you are not currently leveraging mobile marketing to promote your business, you will soon be left behind by the fast-movers and early adopters of this powerful technology. All businesses will have a Mobile website and Marketing is essential for the growth of your Business!

Are You Ready For Mobile Marketing?

There are many factors that you should consider before jumping into mobile marketing for you own business. Even if you have enough money to invest, understand all of the privacy issues involved in mobile marketing, and think that you're pretty much good to go brand new with this technology, you should first consider the type of business that you own, and your specific promotional need. Let's discuss the major kinds of businesses and then we'll discuss key points to help you know if mobile marketing is really right for you and your business.

The Kind of Business You Run Matters

What kind of business are you in? Are you an online retailer, or an offline brick and mortar company or both? Are you a services provider or a product merchant? Are your goods tangible, such as shoes, clothes, books? Or are your goods "virtual" in nature, such as e-books, software, or online subscriptions?

Statistics show that businesses that operate with online goods and services tend to have a higher response rate with mobile marketing. This does not mean that only online businesses with electronic goods and services should use mobile marketing. It simply means that because of the already existing online platform that the business operates on, that mobile marketing can be a very effective way for that business to grow and increase revenue.

Individuals who provide online services, such as internet marketing consultations, copywriting, article writing, e-books, online news subscriptions, and forum memberships tend to have a higher chance at success with mobile marketing. This is because their target market is already used to using the Internet and is very likely to be using their cell phones to access forums, blogs, and the kinds of things that are being sold.

On the other hand, offline businesses can still benefit greatly by using mobile marketing. For instance, restaurants, retailers, automotive repair shops, beauty salons, realtors, chiropractors,

Dentists, etc. can all use mobile marketing very effectively to promote their business. Do you have a special offer, coupon, or discount that would apply to your business? Chances are your customers will be very receptive to receiving messages from you to let them know that this is the case.

Businesses whose cater to an older demographic may not do so well with mobile marketing. Although mobile phones are very popular with young and old alike using

Them, the truth is that the older generation above 35 years of age still is not very comfortable with the current cell phone technology.

Many of these people are likely using older model cell phones that are not smart-phones and may not be able to pull up mobile-ready websites. Many of the older models being used today don't even have internet access.

Even those that do have access to the Internet on their cell phones may not be comfortable enough with the technology to respond to your marketing messages.

For example, businesses such as diabetic supply companies, denture manufacturers, and any services and products geared towards the 50-plus market may want to seriously consider if mobile marketing is going to be worth the time and money. It does not mean that the older generation does not use cell phones or the Internet. It simply means that there are more challenges with this market in terms of mobile advertising methods.

Another point to keep in mind is the action that you want your target market to consider after receiving your mobile marketing messages. Do you want them to come to the store and buy something? Do you want them to respond by email? Do you want them to call?

Because the cell phone is a very personal item to your audience, you really want to be sure that you have a complete sales or marketing funnel in place. In addition, you want to be sure that you have as many tracking and measuring features in place. This enables you to understand the mobile marketing phenomenon closer and helps to avoid costly mistakes in the future. One of the most costly mistakes is antagonizing or angering your market by sending them unwanted marketing messages to their cell phone. This is a very unforgiving arena, so thorough knowledge, planning, and communication is vital, lest you inadvertently damage your brand.

Mobile Marketing Madness
Strategy and Devices

Depending on your specific business and the products and services that you sell, your mobile marketing needs will be unique and tailored to this particular model.

There are several different aspects of mobile marketing that you can implement to promote your business.   One of the most popular forms of mobile promotion is text messaging (SMS). Text messages will be delivered instantly to the user's cell phone. They usually tend to be short and concise, and will either direct the person to a website or get them to call your business. With text messages there is not enough room to fully explain the features of a product or service.

Texting It is so powerful because you have to see the text to erase it, but you've seen the message (top of mind consciousness) and the open rate its 100%.

There is also the emotion of email mobile marketing. This is where you send messages to someone's email. Many people use their cell phones to check email; therefore, this can be considered a form of mobile marketing as well. As with text messages, you're marketing messages need to be short and concise.

Another form of mobile marketing is in-game advertising. This is where individuals are using their cell phones or portable gaming consoles to play games. The marketing is done within the games. These messages need to be short and highly relevant, as the gaming marketing is very unforgiving for spam and interruptions to their gaming experience. If you decide to use this route, you need to be sure to thoroughly understand the gaming market and experience. If you don't, it is advised that you use a consultation of a gaming advertising network.

Mobile Apps is another Avenue that can put you in front of your customers if you want to give Services or Games of some sort. There is monthly cost involve, however there is a huge opportunities in this market. We have done this and customers go wild for your own Mobile App.

Types of Cell Phones

There are many different types of cell phone models on the market today. It all depends on the customer's needs and desires. There are web capable cell

Phones, such as the Blackberry personal assistant, camera phones, digital phones, analog phones and the list goes on. Most individuals in today's age only want a simple gadget for emergencies. Others want all kinds of features on their phone, including being able to record video footage and change the television station. Some cell phones even come with features that can measure your heart rate or tell you how many calories you've burned when walking or exercising. It's a Smartphone and Computer wrapped in one.

They also seem to have an RFID tag that helps to track the location of the cell phone. In addition, there are many different kinds of plans. Some of these include a free phone, while others charge for all kinds of extra features. Customers who want to use camera phones will most likely take a lot of pictures with it. This is excellent for photography businesses that may be able to offer their goods and services to camera cell phone users.

Major Types of Cell phones

Conventional Cell Phones – Standard cell phone models typically sell from $19 to $299, and they are often given away with a contract for two years. Prepaid cell phones also fall under this category. They are rapidly becoming an alternative solution to the expensive cell phones.

These kinds of phones are usually small, light and compact. They have a keypad and don't take a lot of time to learn how to use. They also enable you to store important phone numbers, receive and send text messages or SMS, and of course enable you to make phone calls.

A large number of conventional cell phones are also equipped with cameras and wireless Bluetooth support. In addition, there is an option for hands-free headphones. A large number of them are also able to access high speed

Internet network, so that you can watch videos and listen to music. There may even be a touch screen available, a browser, QWERTY keyboard, memory card slots, and a mega pixel cam.

Smart phones - These are cell phone that come with an organizer, can handle multiple email accounts, and can manipulate office files. Many of these even enable you to use spreadsheets that are supported by Microsoft. The screen display is usually larger, so you can easily use the touch screen feature. In addition, their cameras are usually more sophisticated than those on the conventional cell phone. They may also include wireless data networks, WIFI ability, and internet browsing. The operating systems are usually more advanced and enable users to access shopping, games, productivity tools, maintenance tools, news, travel, weather, finances social networking and more.

Some cell phones are small and compact, while others are big and bulky. This will make a difference in the kind of person or market you're going to be dealing with. Some individuals prefer the flip cover phone, because it is usually small and compact. This makes it easy to fit into a pocket or a woman's purse. Other people prefer the larger phones for easier access. Video phones and camera phones enable people to capture various images and moments. The T-Mobile Sidekick is one such product that enables video capture and has a lot of various features. The more popular cell phones are Kyocera, Ipad, Motorola, Sony Erickson, Nokia and Sprint.

It is important that you take the time to inform yourself about the various cell phones that are available. Certain kinds of customer profiles are directly related to specific types of cell phone usage. An older market would probably have more dated cell phones or they may choose a very simple phone.

Mobile Marketing
Presence & Your Business

Having laid out the various advantages and disadvantages of mobile marketing, it's very easy to see that the upside of this cutting edge technology far outweighs the potential downside. So how to you implement this strategy in your own business to increase your sales and connect with new customers? Choosing the right strategy to reach current and future customers is the key to your success.

For example, simply "mobilizing" your company's existing website does not mean you are open for business. Unless your website or blog is mobile optimized for different cell phones and devices, it will not fit the screen properly. For example, some mobile devices are too small to view standard web-based content, which means the end user must scroll up and down and from side to side in order to find the relevant information about your company's products and services.

In fact, if your site is not optimized for mobile devices it may not load up or be viewable at all on a small cell phone screen. If the site is not navigational a potential customer will quickly exit and move on to another site....possibly a local competitor of your business!

And with literally billions of people searching for information on mobile devices every day, it's apparent that if your company's website is not mobile-optimized, you could be losing out on a lot of business.

We do a simple Mobile detection and take care of this issue that's arising in the Google Search engines because there are lots of savvy Customers looking from there smartphone..

Customers don't like to see website all bunched up together or takes more than 3.5 seconds to load up on their smart-phones.

Also if you have Flash website and you spent thousands on your site, the smartphone won't even see that! I have Clients and Doctors spend 10,000. - $20,000. On their Flash sites and now you're losing tons of customers... Let's have a closer look at a few reasons why your business should have a mobile website.

Key to the Growth Madness

A key to the enormous growth of mobile phones in the past several years is the fact that they are so handy and portable, and can be taken with you anywhere you go. In fact, most people have a mobile device within arm's reach 24 hours a day.

Why? Well because of the portability and robust search capabilities of today's devices, they have to a large extent completely replaced traditional laptops or desktop computers. As a result, you will see people using mobile devices at work, shopping, sporting events and while stuck in traffic. Therefore, to maintain the proper mobile presence with today's consumers, a mobile optimized website is essential.

Today's smart phones allow you to download special "apps" to be able to access Google and Yahoo, allowing the ability of being "found" in on page one of these search engines for local search results related to your business and location. Of course, if your site does not render properly because it is not mobile optimized, this ability for consumers to connect with you via these search engines will often do you no good, resulting in the potential loss of a new customer.

Having a "mobile-friendly" website for your company simply means that new customers will be able to find you from wherever they are searching if there on the go. You will be able to meet them wherever and whenever they are at online, and they will be able to obtain the information that they are searching for since your company's website is formatted properly to their mobile device.

Most will simply be looking for contact information like your telephone number, address, directions to your place of business, or the specific products and services that you offer. Therefore the site needs to be up to date and easily accessible 24x7 in order to welcome these potential customers.

Mobile Marketing Pros and Cons

Like any dynamic new technology, mobile marketing contains advantages and disadvantages to the new user. In this chapter I will lay out an objective analysis of the pros and cons of this

 technology, so that you can create an informed opinion for yourself whether mobile marketing is a good fit for your own business.

First of all, to the "uninitiated", managing you mobile marketing campaigns correctly and effectively can prove to be quite challenging. There are just so many different variables that can contribute to a bad campaign, as well as to a good one that brings the results you want.

At first glance, you have consumers, advertisers, and carriers in the equation. Then, going further, you have third party networks, such as Quattro, Third-screen, and En-pocket involved. You also have organizations, such as Interactive Advertising Bureau, CTIA Wireless Association, and The Mobile Marketing Association.

These organizations deliver guidelines and resources in order to set high standards in the industry. In essence, they are designed to help the industry progress and advance.

Local mobile search advertising and marketing is not as established as local search marketing is. It is estimated that advertisers and marketers are going to spend $11.5 billion globally on mobile marketing this year.

The actual number of cellular phone users is also expected to advance to over 5 billion this year. In the United States alone, there are over 300 million cell phone subscribers alone.

The number is expected to double next year.

This makes mobile marketing and advertising the next big thing in the marketing community. We seem to be on the edge of a whole new era in mobile technology. However, there are quite a few challenges to be dealt with by the new user.

Let's have a look at both the advantages and disadvantages of this technology.

Pros:

This is high coverage of cell phone devices with two times as many mobile users as PC users.

Internet searches on cell phones will exceed searches done on personal computers.

Mobile technology provides access to many buyers who cannot afford personal computers.

Cell phones are able to receive input at anytime from anywhere. This enables advertising designed for specific locations. It also enables marketing campaigns that are based on buying behavior.

Mobile phones are very personal gadgets that individuals tend to take wherever they go. This makes it very convenient for advertisers to create and nurture a relationship with their target market.

Cell phone carriers have market information, location information and data that can be available for marketing purposes.

Interactivity, immediacy, and personalization of mobile advertisements elicit a response by the user.

Studies show a high response rate for cell phone users. They are usually around five percent click through rates, as opposed to traditional advertisements with only one percent click through rates.

Mobile technology provides new ways for advertisers and marketers to communicate with target markets.

IPhones and smart-phones are designed to really enhance the web surfing option. This of course boosts cell phone marketing campaigns.

Cell phone marketing programs can be specialized and targeted. This makes them a lot more successful than traditional forms of marketing.

Cell phone marketing campaigns are opt-in enabled. This means that the people receiving the advertisements have already shown an interest in the services and products offered.

Cell phone marketing can also assist in building a customer list. Once the individuals have opted to receive marketing and advertisements from your company, you are able to use the information to promote your business further.

Mobile advertising can help to create a buzz about your company, services, and products. Due to the fact that your marketing messages will reach their intended audience while they are socializing, shopping and making purchase decisions, you can experience a much higher response rate.

Cons:

Some consumers have a general distrust and of receiving marketing messages on their cell phone, and consider it a form of "spam".

Many carriers impose a wall that eliminates any unfettered access to the mobile device.

Adaptation of messages and content can end up with inferior

user experiences.

There is a huge scarcity of sites that are mobile ready at this point in time. (Only eight percent of the top one thousand United States brands have a mobile website)

WAP-based mobile technology is low. It does not support any kind of investing in the creation of sites that are mobile ready. This is due to the fact that the volume of traffic is low.

There is a period of trial and error required for those who use mobile advertising and marketing. It is much different than the web marketing.

Marketers are leery of the privacy issues surrounding mobile marketing.

The Federal Communications Commission has yet to make a ruling on the release and use of consumer information. This includes information on location.

In April of 2011, the Federal Communications Commission released information that requires mobile advertisers to get expressed consent from anyone whose data they plan to release. This makes it very easy for the consumer to simply opt-out.

Mobile advertising is complex and very fragmented. This is due to the numerous differences in carriers, cell phone devices, pre-loaded applications, and functionality.

The reach is very low at this time. This is because the content consumption in this area is less than ten percent of the total number of cell phone subscribers.

Penetration of devices with 3G is also very low in most countries around the globe.

The establishment of metrics and measurements that are reliable enough for marketers is still lacking.

There are many more things to know and understand about mobile advertising and marketing methods besides the above listed points. You really want to know what methods work the best, how to effectively segment and target your buyers, and then combine everything into a successful campaign.

Learning About "Going Mobile"

Mobile technology is growing at an amazing rate, and as a result mobile device manufacturers are keeping pace with new and improved platforms and formats. Upcoming new and advanced technologies are defining the path for business and commerce growth. Advanced digital platforms are being developed to help businesses reach new target markets…and in turn create more sales.

Millions of new users are picking up a mobile device every day, and this trend will continue to grow in the coming years. There are currently 5 billion mobile device users all across the globe, and these potential customers are using their hand-held devices to surf, connect, and consume information and services.

So how can you capitalize on this dynamic trend in order to drive traffic and generate sales for your products and services? Here are some tips and tricks that you might consider to "mobilize" you current business and cash in on the mobile trend

1. Become Familiar With Mobile Plug-ins

If you use a blogging platform like Word-press for your current website, then making it mobile friendly be as simple and easy as getting an appropriate plug-in. If you are unfamiliar with Word-press and do not know how to search for and update your company's website yourself, be sure to consult with your web-master. These plug-ins have to be set up correctly in order to work properly, so exercise caution of this if you are doing it yourself.

2. Creating A Mobile Website

If your company's website is not built upon a Word-press platform, then it is an HTML-based site. If this is the case, I recommend that you create an entirely new mobile-optimized site will be accessible to multiple mobile devices. This simply means that when a consumer tries to access your current site from their handheld device, they will be redirected to you new

Mobile-friendly version instead. Again, you will most likely need help from a professional webmaster in order to set this up.

3. Flash Is Not Going To Be Seen On Your Mobile Site, Don't Do It!

I recommend that you do not use Flash-based application on your mobile optimized website, as many mobile devices cannot access this format. And even if they do, it often takes much too long to upload, making it impractical and frustrating for your visitor to leaving your visitor. Remember, your consumer is looking for instant results, and any delay in their ability to quickly access information about your business will typically result in them clicking away, never to return to your site.

4. Mobile Website Needs To Give The Info, Fast and Quick!

Mobile phone screens are small compared to your desktop or laptop monitor. Therefore, when creating your mobile-friendly site you should only include the most important information that you think the user would be looking for. This includes contact information like phone and fax numbers, your email address, directions to your office or store, and your hours of operation.

How to Leverage Text Message Marketing

Technology has changed our lives – especially in recent years. Each day, new ideas are turned into objects that are meant to make our lives easier. As new technologies continue to develop, businesses are forced to keep up if they want to sustain in today's tough economic conditions.

Today's highest means of communication device is the mobile phone. Mobile communications continue to improve as more features and functionalities are added. In contrast, some smart phones are better equipped than desktop computers!

With these reasons, businesses have to start "mobilizing" if they want to really stay in front of their target market.

The most popular form of mobile marketing is the use of SMS Text Message Marketing. What is "SMS"? It stands for "short message marketing, and it gives you the ability to communicate directly to your target market by sending a simple, quick text message. This permission-based program is perfect because your recipients have opted-in to receive your messages. The best part is that it's effective because they WANT to receive your promotions.

SMS text messaging is all about the deliverability of the message. Most are read within minutes of be received. In fact, recent studies show that 97% of text messages are read within minutes of receiving them making this is the perfect way to get your promotions across to your target market.

A benefit of SMS text massaging is that its more time-efficient compared to traditional advertising methods. There are character limits on messages so they have to be short, so putting together your marketing message takes just a few minutes instead of days and weeks to prepare.

You can obtain metrics on the status of your messages as well. You have the advantage of monitoring and finding out what happens with each message you send out since it's traceable.

Can a newspaper, TV, or radio ad do that? NOT AT ALL!

SMS text messaging is a low cost means of retaining customers. These are customers who have already spent money with you, so chances are, they will come back to spend more money with you as long as you keep in touch with them.

There are many different marketing strategies available today for business owners but not all of them are as effective and profitable as a SMS text message marketing campaign. If everything is set-up well and you are taking good care of your list, your business can bring in a lot more money with the use of this amazingly effective technology.

The Right Path to Your Mobile Text Messaging Campaigns

Mobile marketing technology has been instrumental in adding thousands of dollars the bottom line of many business types and

categories. However, just like any other marketing strategy, text message marketing (also known as SMS marketing) must be properly planned and executed in order to produce optimal results.

Firstly, make sure that your text message is succinct and to the point. Ideally try to deep it at a maximum length of 160 characters, as this is the limit for most text messages.

Here are a few guidelines for all of your text messages:

Include Your Business Name

This sounds like common sense, however, you would be surprised how many small business owners forget to even include the name of their business in every text message.

The name of your business lets you brand yourself and your company, and makes all of your messages identifiable to the end user. People want to know exactly who they are receiving messages from, as many mobile device users have to pay for each text message they send and receive. This will put

Them at ease as they know exactly why they are receiving the message and hopefully will make them a repeat customer.

You can do this by listing your company's name should be the "sender", and also by including the name of your business in the body of the message itself.

ALWAYS Give Them the Option to Opt-Out

SMS Text Message marketing allows people to opt-in to your list, which means they WANT to receive your promotional offers and messages. However, there should be an easy way to opt-out of the list if someone really wants to do so. This option to opt-out makes a lot of people feel more at ease when the time comes to opting-in to your list. Don't put the opt out link 2 pages of blank space. Given the option fast and up front. Deal with the right list, responsive and loyal.

3.   Include a "Call-to-Action"

Be sure to TELL people what you want them to do. If you don't tell them exactly what to do…you will rarely get the results that you intend. For instance, if you want them to bring the coupon for a free pizza into your restaurant, tell them exactly how to do it and where your restaurant is located. Call to action is the most important message you have to give as soon as you can. Look at some website and you'll start to see that call to action is most of the time there, now that you know about it, you will see and love the different ways they have the call to action message.

The Right Message to Your Customers Is Essential

Every day millions of Americans use their mobile phones to communicate with each other. In fact, text messaging is becoming more common than phone calls via their mobile devices.

From a business perspective, mobile phones are one of the most essential devices and a necessity to most people. In light of that, marketing business strategies using mobile promotion are being utilized by many businesses to reach out to potential customers – including SMS text message marketing.

For SMS text marketing to be effective and deliver the point, one must be cautious on how you use it. Proper planning is essential when getting involved in mobile marketing in order to get the best return on your investment (ROI). How you portray SMS text marketing has a big impact on the outcome of your goals.

The feedback you receive from people will tell you how well your message is coming across when you try to present your products and services. Therefore, proper text etiquette and creativity of your mobile promotion will greatly affect the amount of attention you will receive.

Here are a few SMS Text Message Marketing etiquette tips that you should follow:

1.   Be upfront

Rambling on about what you are trying to say will only confuse a new customer and likely push them away. So be clear and concise in your message to them. If you want this new customer to actually doing something then clearly state that. This way there is no misinterpretation of what you expect from them.

2.   Use precise language

Your SMS promotion has one chance of relaying a message to the new customer, and only 160 characters to do it. Do not use slang or offensive words that will make the customer feel degraded. And always

Be sure to carefully review your completed message BEFORE you send it out!

3.   Do not be misleading

There are many scams on the Internet these days. Be honest with what you are selling and only state the facts. A bad reputation form false advertising using SMS text messaging will only hurt you in the long run.

4.   Come across friendly and courteous

Being polite and friendly is the best way to start of a SMS text message. It grabs the customer and will keep them interested in the message you are trying to perceive. This will keep them in your list and not force them to opt-out.

5.   Free information is How to grow your list quick

Providing free information is a great way to find a receptive audience to your text messages. Giving away free information, coupons, rebates, and similar promotions will always increase customer loyalty and keep them coming back for more.

5 SMS Marketing Mistakes
That Can Hurt Your Business

Mobile marketing is one of the most cost-effective online promotional strategies for one simple reason: because it gives businesses the ability to reach a targeted audience wherever they are.

They no longer need to be tethered to a home-based computer in order to receive information. Billions of people use mobile devices every day, so the correct mobile marketing strategy will allow your business to capitalize on this enormous potential customer base. Unfortunately, many businesses today are NOT utilizing the full capability that mobile marketing offers to increase profits and ROI.

Are you looking for a way to build a massive list of loyal customers that are seeking out your company's products and services over and over? Then here are a few SMS text message marketing mistakes you need to be aware of and avoid at all costs

Not Including a "Call to Action"

If your text messaging does not contain a call to action then you are really missing the boat. What is a call to action? It can be as simple as saying "Click here for more information". If you don't tell your prospects exactly what you would like them to do, chances are they won't take any action at all…and a valuable opportunity to have them opt-in to your list, or discover more information about your products or services is squandered

No "Carrot" For Signing Up

Everyone loves a bonus. So an effective marketing strategy is to offer your potential customers a valuable sign-up bonus as incentive to join your list. This can be an instant reward like a coupon. For example, you might send a text message that says "Show this text message to Fancy Pizza today for 10% off your order price". Many people travel with their mobile devices; this is an effective way to increase foot traffic into your store or restaurant.

Spamming Your Subscribers

Many customers love getting text messages like the one above, but hate feeling like they are being spammed. You must be mindful to scale your daily texts to an acceptable rate. Too many might force the user to opt-out of your list forever, which is certainly counter-productive to your mobile marketing campaign. Text messages sent once or twice a month will keep the customer anticipating your next special deal, and keep their interest high in your marketing campaign.

No "Thank-You" Incentives

Because you want to keep current customers happy and wanting more, you don't want every message that you send to them overtly be a promotional in nature. An effective way to accomplish this is to offer "freebies" to your subscribers every now and then. These can be simple like sending a text message that says "FREE STUFF - 2 days only!" or "1/2 off all purchased items". Your list needs some exciting offers to keep it fresh.

No Strategy for Referrals

It's important to tap into the viral nature of the internet. To do this you will want to have your customers sharing information about you and your business with their friends and family. Therefore your offers of and services MUST have a "Refer a Friend" system implemented. Give you're "referring" customers a nice reward for referring others and watch your list (and your bottom line) quickly grow. A satisfied customer will very likely refer your site to a friend if you give them an opportunity.

Learn About QR Codes and Why the So Consumable

Today, large companies are incorporating the exciting new technology of QR codes in their overall marketing strategy, and they a perfect fit for mobile marketing. "QR codes" stands for Quick Response codes which were originally created by Japanese car manufacturers for the purpose tracking down car parts. Today, they are gaining popularity all over the world because they offer consumers the ability to quickly scan information and data with mobile devices.

These QR codes are distinctive, consisting of specially patterned

black squares against a white background. Data is embedded with these codes and accessed via a click with a mobile phone. Business can utilize QR codes to support product discounts, special offers or to promote new coupons or to send them to your web page, Facebook fan page, or any other web property.

Here are some ideas that you can use to leverage the power of QR codes in your own business:

1.   No Printing Costs

One benefit of QR codes is that you do not need to reprint advertisements or flyers every time you change a particular promotion. Simply clicking to QR code will trigger your mobile phone to go to the source and pull down the most current information about that product. Your customers can therefore click this exact same code anytime and get the most up to date information.

2.   Enhance Customer Excitement

Adding QR codes to your product line will add a new layer of excitement for the customer. They will want to scan your image to see if anything has changed since the last time they clicked your image. This information will appear instantly and the customer will feel satisfaction which will help grow your business.

3.   Quick Response

The best thing about these "quick" codes is that they represent instant delivery of information at the point of sale. This means that the consumer no longer has to wait to get home, turn on their desktop computer, etc. in order to research your product or service. At the end of the day, QR codes facilitate immediate access to information about your business, products, and services, which make them an invaluable addition to your mobile marketing campaign.

QR codes can also be used to conduct surveys and obtain customer feedback about your product or service. And even though QR codes are still fairly new, consumers already recognize and are using them in magazines, websites, brochures, and even in retail stores.

QR Codes in Your Own Business Will Grow Like WIld Fire

Marketing and advertising can be very expensive, but without these activities, how will your business grow? The fact is that

marketing and advertising are the life line of your business. Many businesses simply neglect to invest enough time, money and energy in advertising, and often they often pay the ultimate price: an "Out of Business" sign hanging on the front door.

Many small business owners make the mistake of thinking that by simply having the highest quality product or service; people will automatically come knocking on their door. This couldn't be further from the real truth...in fact; customers simply want to know why they should purchase from your business instead of from your competitor.

So just what can a "QR Code" do for your business? Below are five examples of how you can immediately incorporate QR codes into your current marketing strategy:

1.   Social Platforms

With the popularity of social media, QR codes can be added to your business web pages or social media profiles such as Facebook. This will

Give potential customers the ability to instantly scan your codes and connect to the information they are seeking.

2. Business Cards

Another means of using QR codes effectively is adding the code to your business card so the customer can connect directly to your company's website, Fan-page, or any other online promotion that you wish.

3. Product Packaging

If you deliver packages to your customers, QR code can be used to direct them to online manuals or presentations on how to use that product...A simple but effective strategy that can be easily implemented with a sticker applied to the package.

4. Electronic Press Releases

The power of an online press release can be multiplied by incorporating the inclusion of a QR code. Once you have the customer's attention and wanting more, they will notice the QR code at the bottom of the page and click that image. Then you can take them to a larger article or a web page that promotes that product you just described. The possibilities are endless.

5. All Printed Promotional Material

Branding your business and products can be greatly enhanced via QR codes, and many businesses are adding them to all printed promotional materials and advertisements. In fact, you may have already noticed them yourself on postcards, billboards, magazine ads and in newspapers. This strategy allows businesses to easily target your customers with specific information that will keep them coming back for more. Remember, throwing in freebies is also a powerful marketing concept that keeps them coming back for more.

QR Codes (Quick Response) Are Awesome for smart-phones access you can scan these QR codes from your smart-phones and be taken to a Website and other functions to lots of destinations.

QR codes you can put it all over the place from 1000 Pizza boxes to big Billboard signs in NYC there a quick awesome way to get your customers download information, coupons, a V-card, URL and so many other things. We have a Video on our site www.NuMarketingSolutions.com

There are many apps that you can download from your smart-phones Apple has created the Apple Store and there over a Billion downloaded Apps in 2012.

Many clients have taken their Mobile Application and have put their business and have been very successful.

The possibilities are endless

Mobile Coupons to Go Will Explode Your Business

Okay, here's a fact of human nature: people love "freebies", and the idea of getting something for nothing is irresistible to 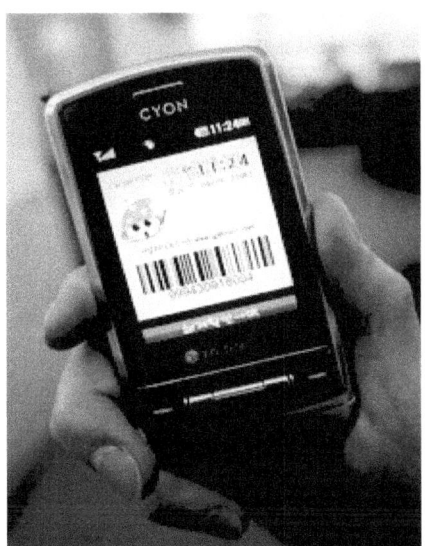 consumers. This idea can be easily incorporated into your mobile marketing campaign by offering discounts and coupons that customers can access directly from their handheld devices.

However, don't just offer freebies or discounts willy-nilly...rather, a considered and systematic approach is necessary in order to achieve the best results.

Think very carefully about what services you can afford to let go at a discount (or not charge for at all), while at the same time keeping in mind what your customers want and need the most. For example, many businesses offer free pens, magnetic stickers, or note pads with their company's logo printed on it. And while this may seem like money well-spent from your standpoint, these gifts usually do not have much promotional value to your business from the consumer's perspective.

In some cases, useless freebies may actually cheapen your business image, and can even offend your market. A really great way to use coupons is to gather a list of previous customers who have spent money on your products and services. Sending them coupons or discounts on future purchases can add to customer loyalty.

Traditionally, coupons are printed in papers and attached to magazines and newspapers. But the traditional paper coupons are quite costly since it involves paper and printing materials. They also can be expensive in that they have to be mailed. Postage is usually very expensive.

This is because most people have their cell phones with them at all times. Once they receive an SMS with a coupon, they are much more likely to open it. The chances of a response or an action are also greatly increased.

Many Americans own cellular phones and many of them, or perhaps most of them, always carry their mobile devices with them.

They tend to carry them to work, to play, shopping, running errands, almost everywhere they go. Therefore, your SMS coupons are likely to be read by consumers just minutes after your send them out.

What does "mobile marketing coupons" really refer to? It is one effective way of reading out and connecting with your target market by means of a "tried and true" method – the coupon. Your promotion will be received fast without having to scan papers and wait for monthly magazine issues. Unlike the traditional paper coupons, mobile coupons are not easy to lose.

Imagine getting an SMS with a coupon to your favorite store. Let's say you're a musician and you play the bass guitar. Guitar Center has just sent you a coupon for 30% off all bass strings. You see the coupon and the next day you make your purchase with the discount.

It is a lot different than ordinary coupons that have to be cut out of the magazine or newspaper, then stored or saved until it is time to go shopping. SMS coupons also don't require shuffling and sorting, like ordinary coupons do. They can be used instantly, right there from the phone.

In addition, SMS text coupons are more unique and compelling, and will therefore convert much better than Paper coupons.

In fact, SMS coupons have been shown to outperform standard paper coupons by almost 2 to 1. There is also the viral nature of a "virtual" coupon, as they can be instantly shared among a prospect's friends and family. Mobile coupons are more talked about and shared by many people. In this way, you can instantly add even more people to your mobile list without doing any extra work. And as every astute marketer knows, "The money is in the list".

This is a key secret about the mobile coupon. Traditional coupons have to be cut out and then saved for later use. They cannot be shared by other people, since there is only one coupon per purchase. Mobile coupons, if useful, will be sent to all kinds of people. This means that your coupons go very well go viral, bringing in much more business for you.

The concept of mobile marketing coupons is the best way to capitalize on the local mobile market for your business. It shows your businesses existence in the community and that you care to help give back to the customers. It helps increase profits because you are marketing your products and services to a list of customers that WANT your promotions.

Mobile coupons are the perfect way to keep your list active and excited to be a part of your SMS text message marketing list.

Mobile Games and Apps

Mobile technology is growing in leaps and bounds, and not just in the marketing arena. Online gaming has drawn thousands of players to various game platforms. This industry is also moving towards mobile gaming, and while this media may not be a perfect fit for your business, you may consider integrating some aspects of electronic gaming promotion into your own online advertising.

Statistics show that big name corporations are already investing for in mobile gaming in their marketing. An example of this is the Coca-Cola Company. It launched a game called "Thumbs up Everest". This game was a rock climbing adventure.

It came with a prize on a weekly basis for those who had the top scores. This resulted in more

Than 350,000 games being downloaded weekly. The term "avergaming" was born. This form of advertising has been a very successful strategy for big name corporations all over the globe.

A Bollywood film by the name of "Jurm" used to create a buzz before the official release of the movie. A puzzle game in the theme of the movie was made available. The very first day of the game's release, over 150,000 downloaded it. By the end of the week the number had jumped to 500,000 people.

The game proved to be a very excellent viral marketing tool. It was spread from all over the globe by word of mouth. Small towns as well as large urban cities had people in them downloading and spreading the game.

Countries in Asia seem to be leading the way for the industry of mobile game marketing. Twenty-eight percent of the users playing downloaded games make

Approximately two to three download weekly. This is according to the Parks Associate's Research.

North America and Europe tend to lag in this respect. Only thirteen percent in Europe download games weekly. The number is even less, at eight percent, in North America. Many more people tend to play the preloaded games on their phones, instead of downloading them.

There is a very strong market desire for more informational services and more entertainment services from personal cell phone services. Studies show that mobile phone users want to be able to do much more with their phones than they are presently able to. Gaming is one of the desires that rank very high.

More powerful cell phone devices, increased investments on the part of game companies, and wider range of 3G networks will all contribute to an enhanced gaming experience. Game downloads really have not been growing as fast as their Asian counterpart. One of the problems is that lower prices need to be met in order to really boost the mobile gaming technology the way it should be.

Is Mobile Gaming Promotion Right for You?

You don't have to be a gaming enthusiast to be interested in this field. It does not require that you know anything about online multi-user games or that you even like games. The main reason you should seriously be interested in mobile gaming is the demographic of the average gamer.

Consider this: mobile gamers download approximately 5 million games monthly. Out of sixteen million players, thirty-five percent are between 18 and 34 years of age, and are male.

This is the most common demographic that is sought by marketers. It is expected that the gaming group will tend to become more diverse in the future. An example of this is females between ages thirty to forty accounting for a large section of the online gaming community. This sector plays everything from shoot-me up classics, retro, casino, puzzles, and solitaire.

Games are a great way to combine marketing and mobile technologies. This is because they offer support for bigger creative productions. An online game will fill the entire screen and can provide marketing or advertising without any competitor for the user's attention and focus.

This is also attractive, because gaming is a favorite free time activity for kids, college students, professionals, and people of all walks of life. Many of these individuals spend many hours playing games. Some of them spend as much as six to ten hours a day playing these games, thereby using a lot of free time to involve themselves in this arena.

During an individual's free time can be a good time to advertise to them, as they usually tend to be much more receptive to various marketing and advertising messages. Because of the complexity of many games, the user's focus is solely on the gaming screen. This is very different from the mind state of the average web surfer, who may have several different windows open, along with their television blaring in the background.

In a recent survey, sixty percent of the users thought games were ideal for marketing. This is probably because the relaxed state of mind makes it easier to make a purchase decision. In addition, around-game projects are a great way to

Create brand awareness and to build customer loyalty without having to disturb the player.

This is important, because interruptions usually cause people to ignore the advertising message. Take for example when you're watching television. Many people simply mute the commercials, change the channel or get up to use the bathroom or rummage through the fridge. However, in-game interruptions can not only cause players to ignore your advertising, they can also end up causing them frustration and anger towards your brand. In essence, the interruption can anchor a feeling of resentment to your logo and brand. This is definitely not something any business would want.

Game Advertising Networks for the Mobile Platform

Before mobile game marketing can really skyrocket, some potential problems need to be worked out ahead of time. Advertising networks with reliable tracking measures, sophisticated targeting, branding and excellent metrics are necessary. In short, a lot of the same features as other online networks have can be expected. This includes retargeting, impression capping, regional advertising, and self-service.

Also, impression tracking that is reliable needs to be in place. With these factors in place, both small and large marketers and advertisers can start tapping into mobile marketing. This is much the same way that marketers are using Google Ad words and Google AdSense today.

In order for in game's mobile advertising to be effective, advertising networks need to support the innovative and unique actions that enable marketers to tap into all of the cell phone features. This includes location-based advertising, click to call, and opt-in's for text message ads. In addition, viral marketing can also help to drive up the value of mobile marketing and advertising. Advertising and marketing solutions need to be able to offer a path of support for all of the newly emerging mobile formats today.

Mobile-to-Mobile Marketing Is Here To Stay

One of the most interesting opportunities for marketers today is the mobile-to-mobile marketing platform. This uses marketing and advertising that is mobile-based to increase sales of games, wallpapers, icons, videos and ring tones.

In a nutshell, these items can be sold exclusively though mobile marketing, due to the fact those conversions are usually instant. Some reports show a click-through rate of as much as fifty percent.

GPShopper is currently employing mobile-to-mobile marketing in order to promote its Slifter software application. Advertisements that are put within the Greystripe Adwrap network tend to access a large audience of gamers.

They also encourage these gamers to go and download the free software immediately. In order to maximize on this, the marketing material is focused on only those who are using cell phones that have Java enabled.

All around the globe, there is really an increasing interest in gaming and being able to use gaming platforms on the cell phone. This provides excellent opportunities for businesses to create in-game advertising campaigns. The biggest factor will be how marketers will take advantage of the growing technology. Also, another factor will be where marketers and advertisers will invest their time and money.

Marketers can capitalize on what's already available. This includes reliable tracking measures, excellent metrics, and engaging mobile phone users. In addition, it is also possible to put some kind of leverage on the gaming momentum.

Privacy Issues with Mobile Marketing

As you're beginning to think about mobile marketing more and more, you need to keep in mind that there are some major concerns for privacy. In order to make your marketing campaigns effective, you need to know as much information about your target as possible. This includes age, occupation, gender, income, location and more. Unfortunately, this information is considered private, thus making it a tricky subject.

The issue of privacy has been raised many times, when it concerns mobile marketing. Customization of advertising content needs to be targeted in order to reach the relevant audience. In order to customize this kind of information, data mining, user profiling, personal data, buying behavior and other information needs to be implemented. This of course raises a concern for privacy.

Many privacy advocates warn that this is an infringement on privacy. Some carriers have been able to work around this by offering cheaper plants and fees in exchange for being able to market to the user. Mobile television could also override the issue of privacy. However, the consent of the user has to be obtained prior to setting such accounts up.

Mobile TV and mobile search both endeavor to gain the user's permission through the initial account set up stage. This means that without permission to release and use the user's information, the user cannot access the company's services.

A new type of device known as Interactivity Mobile Device is on the horizon and expected to outgrow the cell phones of today. Of course this is going to create a whole new world of communications. Unlike the traditional one way radio, newspaper, and television, this new device offers a two way experience. This introduces us to interactive marketing and advertising.   There has already been a lot of success in the Philippines, Japan and United Kingdom.

Ready to Explore the Mobile Marketing Madness?

Will you be able to manage a mobile marketing campaign on your own, or is the time and learning curve too much for you to handle? The answer to that question largely depends on the type and size of your company, and what kind of goods or services you are promoting.

If you are a private consultant with just two to three clients a month, then you could very likely be able to do a lot of your own mobile marketing. This is possible by getting the consent of your customers for their cell phone numbers and clearly explaining to them what you want that information for. Of course any marketing funnel is going to be very time consuming, and mobile marketing is no different in this matter.

How much time do you have to spend on your mobile marketing? You are probably already busy with your business as is. Do you have the time to do this you and still work your business? Will your mobile marketing efforts interfere with the performance and quality of your business? These are all questions that you should consider.

Often, when entrepreneurs start off

They do not have the monetary resources to promote their business. This is one reason why you can consider doing your own mobile marketing. It is recommended, though, that if possible, to either hire an in-house staff or outsource your mobile marketing.

A lot of people are already making a substantial income from their online promotions. A large portion of these are using search engine optimization to direct web traffic to their social media sites or affiliate offers. They are using social media to attract new clients as well, and growing their in-house mailing lists. How are you currently building your own online business? You are most likely looking for another way to advance it; otherwise you would not be reading this book.

Mobile marketing is considered the next wave of untapped money. It is just getting warmed up and is bound to be the next big hit for all kinds of advertisers. There are only a handful of areas that enable you to capitalize on this growing market at this time. New standards are being developed and created on a daily basis. As a result, there are bound to be entirely new communications systems and media systems

That will enable advertisers, marketers and providers of content to meet online and exchange resources.

There is one area that enables you to use direct messaging at this time. These are known as mobile communications services.

You will be able to develop content, send it out as a broadcast and create discount coupons that can be instantly sent to your customers or market.

The industry of mobile advertising right now is still in the stages of infancy. At this time, you're getting in on the ground floor, so to speak. Mobile marketing is here to stay and there is no stopping the change this has put in the business world.

Hiring an In-House Staff

If you have the means and resources to hire an in-house staff to do your mobile marketing, then this would be a great idea. It means that you will have time to take care of crucial business aspects to keep your business running smoothly, while at the same time having the benefit of an entire team working for your mobile marketing campaigns.

There are some things to consider when hiring an internal staff.

One thing to keep in mind is that individuals may not be as technologically savvy as you may think. For example, you've just hired a 23 year old out of college. He's got a laptop, a smart phone, a Facebook and Twitter account and he's very smart. That must mean that he knows about social networking and mobile marketing, correct? No. Not necessarily.

The truth is that it is amazing how little students at universities and colleges know about their own personal computer technology. They are able to log on to MySpace and Facebook without any problems, but they just don't have the understanding of the principles behind such technology, such as managing and sorting files.

Many classes simply ignore or give very little focus to this area. The same problem exists with businesses who want to use mobile marketing, and who think that because they have a Facebook account and the latest cell phone that they know everything. It is not enough to have a social media account and a cell phone. There is more to it than that.

Back in the early days of computers, there were many commands that were necessary. Now, we have the one click option. This seems to do away with all the different processes of planning and work. Software is created and designed in such a way that it sells services and products instead of helping to accomplish any objections or mission. Therefore it requires the skill of a professional to be able to understand how to leverage and use the technology so that the marketing goals of the business can be accomplished.

Some businesses will hire marketing staff, based only on the fact that the individuals have a Twitter or MySpace account. They assume that the people are able to use social media successfully as a marketing method.

There are many people that have been hired to work on these methods, with just their own Facebook account as a requirement.

The truth is that most of these applications are freely available to hundreds of thousands of individuals, but very few of them are actually proficient in the use of these social media applications and platforms.

This also goes beyond the social networking arena. Even IT directors have problems being proficient. Some may not even know or understand how to gather IP addresses for company resources. They may also get hired on the basis of having a Facebook account. Some company principles consider MySpace and Facebook to be technically challenging platforms and will assume that anyone who has one is qualified for the job.

Many companies are shocked to discover that mobile marketing training cannot be started until the in house marketing staff is first trained in the core fundamental skills that are required first.

So before you fall for this trap, be sure to hire efficiently.

If you want to hire someone for a particular position, but you don't have the information available to make a sound decision, go ahead and seek the help of a consultant.

A consultant is able to help you identify people who are qualified and legitimate.

Don't assume that your staff will figure it all out. Many businesses hire an in-house staff thinking that they will eventually figure it out. When times are time economically, many businesses tend to make a consolidation of the various job duties. They expect one single individual to learn all kinds of skills that may be related.

However, just because your worker is skilled in IT does not mean he is a graphic designer for HTML coder. Even if the person is able to build a website for you, it does not mean he is able to design it, market it and set up a tracking campaign.

Very often, they are too busy trying to handle the routine and daily tasks involved in their original job position, that they just don't have any time for studying, learning and reading in order to become proficient in learning new skills.

Hiring an in-house staff can be quite tedious and challenging.

It can take you away from your priorities. This is especially the case with small businesses and entrepreneurs that may not have a human resource department.

It is not easy to spend time finding out what the job requirements are for a position and then searching for someone to fill that position. Assuming that they will figure it out after you hire them can cause trouble in the future. It is doubtful that this will happen, since he or she is going to be managing a diverse variety of job duties in such a way that he or she is not able to excel at any particular thing.

Your employees need to learn something and then get the resources and support that they need to learn it. This needs to be an initiative at work and not after work. Real targets and goals need to be set, so that your worker has incentives to master the skill.

You should also be realistic about the goals and expectations set forth. It is not wise to expect your new hire to learn how to use Google Analytics if he is a web designer. Individuals tend to do best with at-work training programs, especially when the goals are clear and they have enough training resources to work with.

If your business has a need, it is wise to clearly identify it.

Then, once you've identified it, you want to make a commitment to getting the need filled. You'll want to hire a consultant to help you make educated decisions. Once you hire someone, you'll want to set initiatives in place.

Be sure to give them a reasonable amount of time to

complete them and they provide them with enough time and resources to complete the task. The investment is   short-term, but the benefits are long-term.

Outsourcing Your B2B Mobile Marketing

Should you outsource? That is the magic question. A very common way to decide if you should outsource is to decide what you're at good at and then outsource all the rest to someone else. What is your core competency? Of course this sounds very simple, but in reality it is much more challenging. The crucial key in determining if you should outsource is to evaluate your business and the goals within your business. How can outsourcing help you to attain your mission and goals?

When making a decision to outsource, some things like health insurance, printing, legal consultations and services are going to be very obvious factors. Many businesses outsource these things. But there are some aspects which are not that obvious. Many individuals and business owners, for instance, will outsource their tasks depending on their own core competencies.

For example, if you have a legal back ground, you could handle much if not all your own legal issues. If you have a tax back ground, you could handle your own taxes. This does not mean that you should do your own if you have the skills; it just means that you could.

Many business owners with a legal background still choose to hire an attorney.

Another example is that many business owners are able to create a basic web page, and design their own graphics. The difference is in the result that comes along with doing something yourself and hiring a professional to do it. In addition, there are things in your company that you may not want to outsource. This may require that you keep your attention on these aspects at all times. This includes your cash flow, customer interactions and other things.

Alternatively, other areas just make sense to be outsourced. You can do this initially and then as the business grows, decide to bring in an in-house staff at a future date. If you're not experienced at hiring a receptionist or secretary, then you could simply outsource that to a temporary agency.

Of course you will have to pay a fee, but you get a lot of value. The workers will come in and evaluate your needs and then screen out individuals until they find one (or more) that is a good match for you.

There is no risk to you. If it does not work out, then you can call the agency and let them know to send another person.

Once you find the right individual, then you can make the decision if you want to hire them on a long-term basis or keep them temporarily. If you decide to make them a regular employee, then you may have to pay a fee to the temporary agency.

You do not have to make a decision to outsource until there is enough work for an in-house worker. One of the benefits of outsourcing is enjoying the flexibility of being able to cut back on workers. You don't have to fire anyone. Think about how it feels to have to tell someone whose livelihood is dependent on your company that they are being let go or that they are now only needed part-time. It just makes things a lot easier to outsource. Another benefit is that you don't have to be an expert in any one arena. You can rely on outsourcing vendors to be the skilled professional.

One of the largest advantages of outsourcing mobile marketing is the possibility of saving a lot of money. This will largely depend on the size of your business and also what projects you are going to be outsourcing. If you plan things and evaluate things thoroughly, you can end up saving a lot of money.

As your business grows, you will continue to go back and think about these decisions over and over. You will change in some areas

One of the draw backs of outsourcing is that you are going to put a portion of your business in the hands of someone else. You will need to ask yourself if you can reasonably trust and rely on this individual. Do you believe that they will be around in the future, and not some fly-by-night business? Will they be adapting to your business needs as it grows and advances.

At the end of the day, the decision to outsource your business' mobile marketing campaign comes down to a single question: what activities generate the most revenue   for   your business, and is it worth your valuable time to do this yourself? Like any new technology, there is a learning curve involved in slogging through the nitty-gritty techie stuff.

In fact, you may determine that your time is better spent following up on leads and generating sales for your business, instead of trying to figure out how to launch a mobile marketing campaign with no prior experience. If this is the case, you may find that it makes sense to focus on the "strategic" aspect of your business, and leave the "tactical" to a consultant who is trained to get results using mobile technology.

If you so decide to go with a professional mobile marketing consultant make sure that they present you with a realistic proposal that is designed to create results for you and your business.

5 More Proven Internet Strategies
To Explode Your Local Business Sales

1 Video Marketing

Would you believe that there are over 26 BILLION videos viewed per month in the United States alone? What's more, YouTube is the #4 search engine on the internet, which means that right now somebody is likely searching for your services online in the form of a video.

Imagine if you had the budget to run infomercials 24 hours a day, 7 days a week…you'd dominate your market! That's the power of video marketing.

Let me show you how this is possible on a shoestring (even in a terrible economy!), and be able to engender more trust and respect with your customers than ever before.

2 Lead Capture and Follow-up Campaigns

Did you know that an even GREAT webpage will only convert 5% of its visitors to a purchase? It's absolutely true, and this means that 19 out of 20 visitors to your website are destined to surf away into the ether…and likely find your competitor's website instead.

However the AVERAGE page that offers consumers free information in exchange for their contact info gets 35-40% conversion.

Imagine being able to instantly increase your return on leads 7-FOLD, and do it with push button automation. This is possible, and I can show you how.

3 Local Search Visibilities

Did you know that 30% of all searches online include a city or local term (like "Milwaukee Plumbing Contractors")?

This means that every search for every term will have the local companies that have figured out how to get listed in all of the local directories.

And it goes without saying that your customers can't hire you if they can't find you online. I can make sure that your local business is **found** on Google...for all of the keywords that you need to rank for so that your neighbors can find you online.

4 Social Media Marketing

With over 400,000,000 members, Facebook is a giant that cannot be ignored. Social networks have changed the way people research and make buying decisions and if your business does not have a presence on Facebook, Google Plus, Twitter, and Linked In, you are at a competitive disadvantage in your marketplace.

When leveraged in your favor, social networks like these allow you the opportunity to build more trust, respect, and credibility than ever before.

Imagine being able to have feedback on how to improve your business, and sell more on a daily basis. Imagine being able to turn every customer into a potential raving fan who will advertise for you. I can make it happen, and you can secure my services exclusively in your local market.

5 Blog Marketing

Did you know that 77% of all internet users follow one or more blogs? If you're not capitalizing on the growing community, you're missing out on huge business.

Bloggers are passionate about sharing, and if you have one as a client and can turn them into a raving fan, they can propel your business to new heights.

Let me help you create and manage your video blog, all with push-button simplicity so you can leverage this influence-engine giant for your benefit...And increase your bottom line year after year

ABOUT THE AUTHOR

Certified Online Marketing Expert
consultant, Coach
Direct sales strategist
Speaker
Blueprint Vision Specialist

Derby Valentino Perez is an expert at helping Medium to Large businesses/ Corporations gain a dominant position in their local or nationwide marketplace.

Derby specializes in helping entrepreneurs and small to Medium businesses gain a competitive advantage in their local market both online and off.

"Derby Valentino Perez is a highly sought after consultant and coach to businesses big and small.

He typically charges $250 an hour for a telephone consultation. However he is passionate about local business marketing, and so he is extending a very limited opportunity for a complimentary 30 minute consultation to see if any or all of these strategies outlined in this book will apply to your business."

If some parts of this book seems overwhelming to you, RELAX... Give me a call.

"If you would like to contact Derby for a consultation, you must first call our Customer Hotline Number at 201-575-4200. This is a voicemail system and is never answered live. Or Derby@NuMarketingSolutions.com

When prompted, please leave your name, business name, website URL, and telephone number.

This information will then be transcribed and sent to his assistant

Fabiola Barrios, who will review your request and contact you to schedule a time for the consultation."

He makes sure that these businesses are able to be "found" on the internet, with top ranking in Google, ensures that they never run out of leads, and helps them to transform these potential clients into

Lifetime customers (and raving fans!) There's lots of useful information at Derby's website atwww.NuMarketingSolutions.com

For a Complementary PDF report on "How to get on Google for Free" Go To:

http://numarketingsolutions.com/FreeReportFromDerby

www.ingramcontent.com/pod-product-compliance
Lightning Source LLC
Chambersburg PA
CBHW051223170526
45166CB00005B/2012